To See What Rises

To See What Rises

Poems by Alison Stone

CW Books

Published by CW Books
P.O. Box 541106
Cincinnati, OH 45254-1106

ISBN: 9781625494252

Poetry Editor: Kevin Walzer
Business Editor: Lori Jareo

Visit us on the web at www.readcwbooks.com

Acknowledgements

Thanks to the editors of journals where the following poems, some in earlier versions, previously appeared:

The Bezine – Insurrection Snapshots

Big Scream – It's Easy to Love the Past, Between the Devil

Comstock Review – Daedalus

The Crazy Child Scribbler – "The Future Isn't What It Used to Be"

Diode – Heart

Earth's Daughters – Grandpa Perry (titled Grandfather)

First of the Month – Black Star, Stores Sell Padded Bras for Toddlers, December, There is No Gun, Poem for Kendrick Castillo, Why I Didn't Report, 8 Minutes 46, Seconds (titled Nine Minutes), But Not His Name (titled July 2020), America Hunkers Down, Newt Gingritch Claims 150,000 Dead People Voted, Insurrection Snapshots, Is Beauty Enough?, Quarantine, Still (titled Covid, Still).

Folio – The Plan

The Main St. Rag – Alcestis, Chagall's Bridal Pair at the Eifel Tower

Pink Panther – Leda, Antigone

Pirene's Fountain – July, 2018

The Raven Chronicles – Home, Upstate

Ribbon: Tanka Journal – Late April

San Pedro River Review – Train

Scoundrel Time – People Have Started Saying "Nip it in the Butt"

Shot Glass Journal – Turning Fifty in Spring

Slipstream – March Burial, Rattling, After Vesuvius, A Blood Test Reveals That I'm CT, After the Doctor Appointment

Spectrum Literary Journal – Demeter Clarifies

Stone Canoe – Hudson River Mile 28

Sweet Tree Review – Elegy

September 11, 2015 appeared in the anthology *Never Forgotten: 100 Poets Remember 9/11* (Lulu.com, 2020).

America Hunkers Down and What if I Admit I Like It appeared in the anthology *A 21ˢᵗ Century Plague: Poetry from a Pandemic* (University Professors Press, 2021).

Herd and What If I Admit I Like It appeared in the anthology *The Power of the Pause* (Wising Up Press, 2022)

Thanks to everyone who supported me during the writing of this book, especially Michael, Jessy, and Vee. Also gratitude to readers who helped make these poems better, the talented members of Zoom Poets International and the One O'clock Poets. Also to Faye Rappaport DesPres for editing suggestions. And to Jenny, whose daily phone calls make me better and happier.

Contents

But Not His Name

Spring was lost to lockdown. Now it's summer,
the air thick with humidity and fear.

Returned to work, we sweat into our masks.
The scientists are taken off the air.

I AM NOT A RACIST, the racist yells
while bodies pile up like bags of gold.

Cars honk for protestors carrying signs.
The ground trembles when stone generals fall.

It's always about who has the power.
Years ago, at Ellis Island,

my grandfather, but not his name, allowed
to enter. Boats of Jews turned back to die.

What does it mean
to be American?

Official fireworks banned, my neighbor
provides a noisy, low-budget display.

Zimmerman autographs bags of Skittles.
Fake stallions watch through moss-covered eyes.

Grandpa Perry

I barely knew you
but named my daughter Peri
for my father's sake, remembering vaguely
an overweight, ruddy man
and the details my parents repeated –
bad with money but so generous you fried
giblets for the neighborhood cats.
You took my brother to the barber
his first time, a crew-cut
Mom never forgave.

Is this what life reduces to?
A handful of anecdotes
thinning with repetition
like spinach simmered to wisps.

Some people believe time
is just a metaphor for space,
that each moment still exists,
exactly as it occurred,
the seconds following in a line like beads on a string.

Others think that each choice point
branches like a river, with different selves
taking each possible action.
Maybe the Perry who made savvy
business moves had the ease
and medical care to live long enough
for me to know his jokes,
to have something robust
to tell my girl about her name.

Even if our death date's fixed,
and all that's changeable is how
we get there, still
I like to think of you
somewhere, fedora at an angle,

holding my brother's hand,
my mother smiling as she sees
his neatly-trimmed curls.

Celestial

I don't know how angels feel
about our struggles and hungers,
our fragile, beyond-control
flesh. Did these haloed ones
have bodies once,

and somehow get promoted to gossamer?
Or have they always lived on clouds
of our imagination, listening
to lyre hits as the sky
recycles its blues?

Why do we imagine we'd be happier
up there? Our natures being
what they are, we'd probably gripe
about altitude sickness or envy
the gold in another's curls. Isn't

their satisfied expression what we're
really after, a smug glow
available to all of us
if we could pause and listen
for the beating of wings.

Between the Devil

and the deep blue
of your eyes, I'd choose the pleasure
with the steeper price.
The lack-of-oxygen thrill.
Why venture if there's nowhere sweet
and dangerous to fall?
Nature shows – grab now
before things rot.
Why leave blackberries for some dumb bird
while your own hungers
whirl unheeded in your clenching
heart? We all want rapture's terror,
want to be forgiven and kissed,
stumbling through the world's mix
of *come hither* and thorn.
Knowing the possibilities each day
can hold, the wisest bodies tremble.

Elegy

A suicide in Spyten Dyvel
snarled the trains for hours,
thousands of commutes stalled
by a stranger's pain.

This is death's season, trees'
leaf-flames beginning to extinguish, strappy
dresses packed away.
The time of year you faded.

At your funeral, women stood in turn
to proclaim closeness. Silent, smug,
I sat, trusting the touch
that all these decades later burned.

Though we met when the media
began to warn of lesions,
wasting, cancer – a new penalty for pleasure –
still we spent our bodies in my art school dorm,
so small you joked I'd have to go
into the hall to change my mind.
And I did, fleeing the danger
and delight of us for naïve British boys
and Wall Street hopefuls,
though years of phone calls
kept us loosely joined.

We spoke last after the towers fell.
Numb from the vile smoke in my throat,
I missed the weakness in your voice,
dismissed your fear that pills
no longer kept the virus in check.
Convinced myself you'd rally.

When your niece called and I flew
to your bed, I took off my wedding
band so that the hand holding your limp

and unresponsive one
would be the hand you knew.

After the Break-Up Sex and Broken Glass

I wander through a field of asphodel
whose white spikes whisper,
All desires wane. Thrills fizzle.
The trick's to live diminished
without bitterness. Sleep,
wake, work to outwit bills that spill red ink
across your fantasies. Let your
ringless fingers reach. Kiss
when you can. Find a song that still
spurs you to dance. Every five years
burn your self in effigy
to see what rises from the ash.

Won't Hold

Time of my thinning bones,
of crocus necks broken by snow.
People hiding out in gyms
and skyscrapers, the sun
bleeding day-glow orange
while women type letters in windowless rooms.

Line blurred between satire and tragedy.
Friends sigh,
He'll probably win again.
I just can't pay attention anymore.

Another "warmest day."
Another once-loved #metoo man exposed.
The old myths won't hold.

As we "spring ahead," what rises
from the dark is no lost daughter
but a stranger, feral, smelling of moss,
stumbling among the confused bees,
and even the most stubborn dreamer's
bruised from falling down a flight of stars.

Tunnel

My mind's in a rut.
I tunnel, news-obsessed,
stuck in Mueller/Measles/Notre Dame.
Childhood summers at the beach,
my parents told me if I shoveled deep enough,
I'd reach China, though I always quit
a few feet down to work on my moat
or the sandcastle's walls. *Worry's interest*
on a debt you might not owe,
but that doesn't stop
the incessant repetition. Maybe I should
stop trying to stop and instead
throw myself into the digging
until I reach the China in my mind,
emerge into a mountain shrine,
sweet incense smoking in a bowl, the ancient
face of Buddha urging me to pause
and note the shades of sky.
Travel transforms
and when I return home, even
the news is better – inebriated
but unharmed by CO_2,
the 180,000 bees living on Notre Dame
survived the blaze.

It's Easy to Love the Past

Sun-dizzy summers,
boys' soft, clumsy lips.
Even the indelible worst day
I return to again and again,
clench of shame
drawing my whole body inward and back –
so utter, it comforts.

The present dull as a terrarium.
Bulbous succulents, tumbled rocks.
Exposed behind glass walls, I turn
away from contact. Dissatisfaction
masking fear.

Shall I take a risk? And how?
No vacancy in my heart's best rooms.
The suite marked *friend of*
deepest understanding's filled with you,
ten years gone.

Maybe art can pin me
to *this* grass, *this* murky pond, a clump
of horses grazing, rumps to the wind.

Two colts spook into gallop, strokes of grey
I fail to capture. My sketchbook
fills with lifeless competence.
Most of drawing is seeing, my first teacher
told me, and it's true – my eyes
blurry with nostalgia.

You loved wild horses, blue
silk dresses, jazz. You would have stuck your arm
in this cold pond to grab the sparkling shell
that swells with every ripple.
I try to figure out the light

and surface texture. Stubborn charcoal
crumbles into different shades of *no*.

In your honor, I reach down, gasp
from the water's chill.
Tiny flesh-colored fish dart
from my intrusion.
Fingers grope, then close around
their treasure. What I thought was a shell
is a plastic barrette.

Rattling

After her father died, she longed
for ghosts – strained her ears
toward the cabinets for any
rattling of glass, squinted
upward for a bulb's flicker.
Wished the moans from winter
trees fooled into bloom
by unexpected warmth
meant more than wind.
She knew he could not return
a man, whole-souled,
smelling of tobacco. Would never
wipe mud from his boots and reach out
a broad-fingered hand.
Still, she hoped for some ripple of him
like the O's in a boat's wake,
or a flashbulb's after-image
splashed across her
closed and burning eyes.

Turning Fifty in Spring

Purple splash of crocus, daffodils'
bombastic gold. Bright shoots push
through decaying leaves.
Everywhere the earth unclenches.
My body stiffens, out of sync
with such brash rebirth.

The widower across
the street who stoops to pull
a dandelion sees the lie
in all this spastic blossoming.
There is no starting over.

All in the Family

Those were the days – the family
filing nightly into the den
to watch what the father chooses.

The kitchen and the bedroom, Archie crows,
glowing with blue light.
A common story – good-hearted bigot's
curdled dreams, his nervous wife.
A boy pushing his sister
from the softer chair.
A girl growing like a bonsai.

Ads trumpet odor-masking sprays,
razor blades that cut to the skin.
She likes Meathead, his mustache
thick with ethnicity, and poor
Gloria, whose husband likes her
better with a brunette wig.

She's too young to understand
most of the jokes but knows a father
who earns all the money can sit
while his wife cooks, can spit
Polack and *Dingbat,* call
a married woman *Little girl.*

Her mother leaves to finish the dishes,
missing screechy Edith, hands
fluttering like wounded birds.
Her brother takes the blanket.
Stifle yourself! the patriarch commands.
Her rubbery face collapses
while canned laughter blares.

Likes

There's a name now for what we did
in the nightclubs' dark and on benches
and in beds when the clubs closed –
"hook-up culture." A new book says
the internet's to blame,
that girls post sexy pictures to get attention,
are strung along online by boys
with too many options to commit.

Sweet teen romance
is foreign as another planet
to many of the girls interviewed,
something they crave but
can't imagine having, trapped
in the pursuit of "likes,"
each success or failure measured
and public.

I didn't need technology
to hook my heart to a boy
with a line of wannabe lovers,
each of us competing
for kisses and endearments,
trying tighter skirts, suggestive
gestures, desperate to make him notice.

When my friend switched to girls
and chose an older, distant one,
the insecurity and waiting
by the phone continued.
The always saying *yes*.
We learned a lesson
deeper than gender – the person
with the power was whoever wasn't us.

This Town Was Full Of Cousins

but no one made it safe.
They didn't mean harm,
tying up the girls with pretty ribbons.
Hawks and mothers hovered
while boys, too small to get power
without the help of their bodies,
went on waiting to inflict their cruelty
elsewhere than these copy-cat houses
set back from the street.
God didn't want to see. He went
to some other place.

Upstate

Redolent of Lysol and cranberry candles, our kitchen
makes me miss Manhattan's in-your-face trash.
Though the water-logged air makes subterfuge impossible,
we suburbanites try anyway, prime our punch lines,
practice smiling through both sides of our mouths. Coo
over bruise-colored pansies mottling exhausted lawns.
Next year at this time, we'll be in the same spot
as if frozen, meals and arguments
repeating like a scratched LP. Why did we abandon
our black clothes and move here?
To suck our teeth with big city superiority?
Or because the smog and concrete drained us, not even sex
helping for long? Why is it so hard
to hunker down someplace and make it home,
like the groundhogs happily tunneling
ankle-breaking holes out back?

People have started Saying, "Nip it in the Butt"

Is this a mishearing of "bud" or a mash-up
with "Come back to bite one in the ass," the desire
to breed a new expression from established ones,
the way my daughter's science class imagined
mating superheroes to see which powers the offspring
would get? People who say this seem to be aiming
for the original meaning, "to stop something
in an early stage," though what they're actually advocating
is sexy or inflammatory and would have the opposite effect.
Imagine a speaker, teeth bared, reaching for the derriere
of the situation. Rather than being aborted, it rises,
provoked or turned on, leading the biter to utter
my favorite new phrase, "Oh for fuck's sake," which
my husband hates because "It doesn't say anything" but
which I find perfect for the "War on Christmas,"
thirty-year-old family quarrels surfacing at parties,
being asked, "Can I help you with anything else?"
by someone who hasn't helped me at all,
or the shock of opening the fridge for kale –
which I've always liked with garlic but apparently now is
a sign of supporting "safe spaces" for triggered
college students, as well as being soft on crime –
and having a shelf collapse, splattering our newly-installed
kitchen floor with overpriced organic raspberries and beer.

My Doctor and I Throw Celebrities at Each Other

Why can't the body heal itself?
True, Steve Jobs, who chose juice fasts
over conventional treatment, decays
on my doctor's side, but Patrick Swayze
took chemo and is just as dead.
What about Suzanne Somers,
who cured her breast cancer with herbs
and now has lots of sex?
Or maybe that was a different blonde, the one
whose lover pretended to drown.
The cancer part, I mean – the sex
is definitely Somers. I read about her libido
and bioidentical hormones this morning
while avoiding making an appointment
for a blood test and sonogram.
Why do you fill your head
with crap? my husband asks,
missing the point. I want fashion
and mansions to crowd out
important things. Want to convince myself
the body's so forgiving, a woman
can be flab-free two months after
giving birth to twins. To lose myself in liposuction,
low-cut gowns, and hot affairs. The actors' plumped,
tucked, frozen faces almost making me believe
that they and I might never die.

April, with Corona

Spring sticks to the lesson plan –
blossoms, brash light, gaudy shades of red.
So much new life multiplying,
but the virus has its own math.
Subtraction, division, bodies
in freezer cars waiting for graves.
Close to a school, I used to hear
the children's recess cries, but now there's only birdsong
and sounds of this sudden storm – an odd flipping
between hail and sun-streaked rain –
that drives me inside to screams
from the TV and yowls from the cat.
I want to howl my own prayer
or recrimination, but to whom?
The men in charge are deaf
to voices pitched like mine, and the wind
that shakes my windows isn't God.

America Hunkers Down

Yearning for basketball, friends' hugs,
the gym, we grumble in the space
between denial and loss.

Italian doctors warn
that arrogance protects
as well as prayer.

Soon, the hospitals
past capacity.
The old left to die.

The smog cloud over China's
gone, the canals of Venice
bloom with dolphins and swans.

Will we
lean from balconies
and fill the sky with song?

Is Beauty Enough?

Pink moon hovers above our virus-ravaged town,
where we pose stuffed bears in trees, hoping
to make locked-down children smile.

Spring brings its out-of-sync beauty.
Each day more people sicken. Die.
Isolated, we grieve on screens.

The plague of AIDS
was spread through pleasure.
Now, we fear the pharmacy, the mail,

veer from neighbors as we walk.
Discarded masks bring a new squalor
to gutters. How can we trust this world?

Still, the blossom-patterned grass is safe
under a plenitude of stars,
the full, pink Sprouting-Grass Moon.

Quarantine, Still

Browning magnolia leaves fall
onto discarded gloves. Death
everywhere, if you look for it,
but don't you think the gods are tired
of that same lament?
See, the dogwood is still full,
the tulips newly-opened, the sun
shining like luck. And all that family time!
Your older daughter emerging nightly
from her room to wail, *This is hell. It's hell!*
Your younger clinging to your arm while
struggling with online school.
Your husband fills the kitchen
with laugh tracks and guns. He shows you
his hand, scratched by the emotional support cat,
who preferred her prior role as grumpy pet.
When will we be allowed to step back
into what we were? Or, as in myth,
is transformation permanent? Just in case,
you scroll through masks, decide
whether to change your family's faces
into leopards or backdrops for multi-colored stars.

Quarantine Continues

They have two seasons — Christmas
and America, my daughter notes
about the family whose lawn décor flips
between ornaments and a gargantuan flag.
Right now I almost envy,
though can't fathom, their faith –
in a savior who'll have to rise
alone because the churches closed,
in a country that can't get test kits right.

I taught my kids divinity
is energy in everything,
to cause no harm,
be kind to people, rescue worms.
They lack the comfort
of a god who'll choose to spare them
instead of someone less favored.

So far the new death's once or twice removed –
my brother's best friend's brother,
a coworker's aunt – but they see
enough news to know that no one's safe,
know also that their diabetic father's
especially vulnerable.

The grocery store. The mail.
The man who passed too close.
No god, no government to save us.

Learning M's in the Hospital with Covid

The worst part's knowing you're alone,
the virus too contagious for visitors,
no one to hold your hand
while your smoker's lungs struggle.
(Your cigarettes/my allergies our one recurrent friction)

Though my photos got lost in a move,
for years I kept an envelope of us –
arms around each other in Brookline,
eating chips on a Canadian bridge.
L's party – you in a simple black dress,
me in a silk, pajama-looking thing I thought was chic.
In those pre-selfie days, who snapped the shots?
Your soon-to-be-ex husband? My friend-who-wanted-more?
All I remember clearly from that time is you.

Survivor of so much,
you'll beat this. I can hear
your bossy British voice
demanding it to go.

Still, I wish I could send something
to your room to comfort you –
the blue cloak you lent me
for soul-dark nights,
or your fur coat, which disgusted me
so much, I could barely hug you.
Though you admired my animal-rights fervor,
you wouldn't take it off, explaining
it was a comeback gift from your manager
and wearing it reminded you of triumph.

Herd

Elk on golf courses, bears
in the streets –
with humans on lockdown,
the animals go to town.
Bright spot in the news feed's cycle
of bluster and alarm.

The virus kills by robbing oxygen
from the blood.
African Americans are dying
in higher proportions. *I can't breathe*,
Eric Garner cried. *I can't breathe*,
my client laments, trapped
24/7 with an angry, controlling spouse.
Her suffering is real, though relative.
As is shortness of breath.

With no access to salons,
our animal selves are on display –
shaggy, unwaxed, nails growing unshaped.
With rough hands, we flip from the scientists
and politicians to watch sea turtles return
unbothered, lay their eggs on beaches where
no tourists crush shells or make love.

What If I Admit I Like It

Not illness and death, of course.
Not people bankrupt and starving,
not bills and no way to pay.
Not the crisis, but the quiet –
my dog and I alone on clean dawn streets.
My teen daughters home for every meal.
Time at night to look for patterns in the stars.
Can we keep some of this when businesses open,

or will we barrel forward even faster than before
to make up for lost time?
Will the lions taking naps on roads
fade into myth along with neighbors
joined in song, the smog-gray sky
turned back to its true blue?

Contrast

The birds are at it again,
all flutter and song. Housebound,
Merlin hisses behind glass,
his taut haunches electric with thwarted desire.
Isn't that the season's unspoken subtext?
Spring flaunting sex and renewal, but what about
the lonely, the single, the sick,
made more out of sorts by being out of synch.
The man whose wife collapsed in April
feels in the balmy air the touch of his still-warm grief.
Life's not fair is one of the first lessons
we learn in toddlerhood, as though hearing
this stated by a calm parent would antidote
justified rage. In the tale where the gods
offer to restore her dead baby if the mother brings
a mustard seed from a house untouched by sorrow,
the lesson is that no one is spared. True enough.
But we're afflicted far from equally, and joy's
a fickle guest, despite the weather's demand
for celebration. Better if the world provided rain
for the abandoned lover or too-long unemployed,
a chill for the mother, her bone marrow
not a match, who stumbles
from the drab hospital into the slap of daffodils.

April

Forsythia chant
yellow to the daffodils.
No, they answer. *Gold.*

Shadows of tree limbs
bar the sidewalk. A sudden
breeze opens the gate.

Indoor tabby hears
one bird, louder than the rest,
tease from the tulips.

Leaves shake but don't fall.
The sky blends cobalt, azure,
stripes of airplane trails.

Bright spandex. A clump
of bikers passes. Their words
blend with the birdsong.

Tongue lolling, the dog
bounds after a muddy ball.
Each time the first time.

Adulting Means Getting Out of Bed

The birds are back, spring singing
loud enough to rouse us
from the tangled sheets we wrap in
practicing avoidance, the kind of day
breakfast could easily lead
to dinner in bed.
Season of unabashed wanting,
of eyebags hidden under shades.
If you want to capture someone's attention,
whisper, the perfume ad purrs,
but this feathered jazz band missed the memo,
chirps jamming with squawks and trills,
their industriousness a nudge.
I have to go, I say, and disengaging
from last kisses, do.
Soon a crotchety train agitates me
toward the city, its commerce and warm-
weather bodies on display.
Poor sartorial choices, like that redhead's fuchsia
dress, camouflage beauty, the way a bad rider
hides the skill of her horse.
Fashion's just one flavor of concealment –
language, sex, and religion other ways
to obfuscate, our deepest secrets often
locked away for some rarely-occurring tomorrow.
Some things reveal themselves despite our best attempts,
like a hot butt in tacky pants
or micro-movements of facial muscles
that to a trained eye betray lying or desire.

Friends My Age are Starting to Do Stuff to their Faces

I'm not sure what's more disconcerting –
the pumpkin cheeks or arched, immobile brows
of a botched job, or, when it works,
women in their fifties suddenly smooth-skinned,
looking like they have no kids and spent
the last decade resting poolside
sipping kale juice with a reflexologist on call.
Even a pal who vows she'll never,
one day pulls her sags up, sighs,
I know I'd look much better,
but it's so expensive.
My objection's principle – not
that I'm serene about the furrows and blotches,
but I hope to be, and how can any of us
find beauty in normal aging
if we never see it? My puppy,
joyfully licking my face when I say *walk,*
knows what's important. Nose-led,
she frolics until I jerk her back
from our neighbor's yard, a yellow
pesticide warning sign bright
against the artificial-looking green.
My property's no eyesore. I have the same
forsythia and daffodils. Just as many tulips.
Bleeding hearts to boot.
True, the grass is mottled, but that's
nothing soft lighting wouldn't fix,
or a bright tree to distract the eye
from the fetch path the dog
wore from fence line to stairs.
Let's surrender to my lawn's uneven tones,
accept that thorned vines
wrap themselves around the rhododendron.
And the dandelions are advancing.

Diana Explains about Actaeon

It wasn't modesty, I'm gorgeous,
although aeons older than the stars
you discard at first sag. A goddess
has no expiration date. And no,
I won't titillate you with descriptions
of my eyes or muscle tone. There's
far too much of that in poems.

No boy can reduce me
to a worn-out trope – woman exposed
or shining in the light
of the male gaze.
He needed to learn
how an object feels.

I cast my spell.
I called the dogs.

Demeter Clarifies

My fault, her face closing like a zipper?
Curt wave as she heads out with the giggling
pack, all come-hither hair and bare shoulders,
posing for selfies, smelling like spring.
She doesn't know to fear the boys who "like" her
posts, experts at how to flirt and flatter.
Soon they'll be sending dick pics, asking for
secrets, showing up at our door.

History writes me wrong – a helicopter mother,
scared some punk will sway her child.
The magic that I work's to keep her author
of her own mythology, a wild woman
who can choose, refuse, aspire.
Not some hell-bound object of desire.

Poem Inspired by Ellie Becka's "Many-Eyed Woman"

Argus has nothing on mothers –
the way our vision changes
to be always watching –
window, bookcase, blanket,
each sharp edge, each stick-in-the-throat-
sized charm. Noticing the tiny shifts
in facial muscles signaling
discomfort or hunger.
So much shines as the sun's rays
bounce off furniture and strawberries, pattern
the Labradoodle's fur.
How could I have lived so long
with my two tired, ordinary eyes,
oblivious to all this light?

Shine

Drifting down from birdfeeders my daughters painted,
pooled at the base of valentines - I find
glitter everywhere. Sparkling between one girl's toes,
on my fingers after snapping a bright
clip into her hair. Stray specks
glint on my cheek, my husband's eyebrow. Twinkle
from the cat's fur. Between the laundry and
the squabbles, I pause,
delight in tiny flecks of gold and silver flinging
light to every corner of my blessed, ordinary life.

Warming

The weather's moody
as a middle-schooler – storm and chill,
then unexpected warmth.
Unsure whether to hunker down
or pack a picnic lunch, we ride
the wave, pretending it's a "normal cycle"
that will right itself in the end.
What season's this supposed to be?
my daughter asks. Some times
disaster happens for no reason we can predict.
The car's brakes fail, the baby's
heart stops beating during birth.
Other times the future's obvious as car exhaust
against torn sky. Still, we're all tired
of the polar bear on her melting raft, wide-eyed
and white as a bride.
Holland's been preparing –
building roads that rise
when the dikes break. Here politicians
spoon smooth lies into our eager mouths.
What will we tell our children as earth blares
her angst, and we have no dikes, no Watcher,
Dreamer, or Sleeper to keep
the water-wolf from our door?

Mixed Seasons

Filthy snow mounds shadow
the crocuses' bent necks,

stems of daffodils jaundiced
by out-of-season storms.

Today, more flakes, wind that slices
through my coat. Tomorrow

I'll retire my herbs
to the shelf of wishful thinking

and hand my body over
to Big Pharma. The pills

hum in their bottle –
fifty-six pink moons.

Can death melt like stubborn
snow? The light-soaked

landscape then, so loud
with open space.

Because

Because my daughter wants a poem
without love, death, naked people,
or Persephone
and I can't imagine
what I don't know

Because the radio broadcasts
terror through our rooms

Because sometimes for no reason
I remember Sandra Bland, and cry

Because when regret nuzzles next to me
all night, the dog still
greets me in the morning with her eager nose

Because my daughter and I lift
drying worms from the sidewalk
and return them to soil

Because for all my errors and obstinance
still the mountain offers me the many angles of her face

Because a day can begin with laundry
and end with astonishment

Because if I lie still, the cat
may massage my belly
as though I were dough

Because no war's been averted
by the knowledge that our bones
are made from the same stars

Because my dying friend said she would
contact me, and I won't be fooled
by birds or odd weather

Because I wanted to be broken
and forgiven and healed into shine
but remain messy and yearning and unsure,
my mind a drunken monkey stung by scorpions
despite decades of timed breath
and best intentions

Because while I am willing to ignore
death, naked people, and a goddess, I believe
that love must be allowed in every crevice
it can find a way to enter

Because the dead do not come back

Because birds are only animals
in practical flight
and there are days I can't recall
my mother's face

Black Star

Final London weeks
dancing to Heroes
with my lover
in a nightclub's fractured light,
as our skin shimmered and bodies swayed –
Though nothing can drive them away –
it seemed that Bowie
beat them for us,
his odd eyes
commanding time, transforming
just one day
into a type of forever.

Metro North

Safety is not this railroad's priority,
a flyer on the seat informs me
that an investigation found. Bold
letters designed to reassure blare,
Soon it Will Be.
When? My train should make
Grand Central in an hour.
The slumped man in front of me
starts to snore, then jerks awake
as we lurch around a curve.
A couple argues in German.
I'm hungry, a toddler whines,
and aren't we all, chugging along,
tending the body's circular desires.
The city's close now, smokestacks
rising up like spring's first flowers,
reminding me of when I moved there,
young and ravenous, mesmerized
by the energy, the tawdry glitter,
hoping everything I'd ever craved was waiting.
Safety trivial as sleep.

Heart

You don't have to say good-bye,
reads the taxidermy ad in Cat Fancy magazine,
Keep your loved one at home.
Whom would stiff, stuffed Fluffy,
curled in her favorite basket, comfort?
Yes, the owner would be spared those moments,
common after loss, of walking into a room
and catching a glimpse of the departed, only
to have them morph back into pillow or bag,
but wouldn't the animal's unresponsiveness
sting? Can need blossom
into truth? A woman I met, co-authoring a book
with her dead son – asking questions, listening,
then typing the answers she hears him give – says
she's spared the usual mourning.
The heart wants what it wants,
Woody Allen said when caught
with his common-law daughter,
and who hasn't felt the tug toward what's wrong,
hasn't held a person, grudge, or idea
beyond reason? Though reckoning stands to the side,
licking its lips, we plow
ahead into our pasts' defining hungers,
like an older child craving stroller,
nipple, womb, how later he will
enter a woman and withdraw
into the same grief,
or she will clutch her lover's back
against the crush of morning.
Having learned from the supposedly blueberry cereal,
which dyed our milk grey, the mind's
unfooled by counterfeit but overridden
by the loyal, stubborn, stupid human heart.

March Burial

The snow gave you an extra day
above ground, fear of storm travel
trumping the 3-day rule, though weather
never stopped weekly Boston runs
for your store, son beside you in the truck –
one of many stories that pull you back
from years ruled by your kidney function
and sugar numbers, your wife
reduced to a nurse. Cowed by the bills
stacked unopened during your illness,
you feared "a pauper's funeral,"
but Uncle, there are riches here –
white-gloved marines folding your casket's
flag with the intricacies of Tea Ceremony,
a packed room laughing at your corny jokes.
Your granddaughter's lush alto.
Tales of a bold, playful person I never knew
in our segregated family, where the men
watched sports in the den, leaving the women
to clean-up and conversation.
Though prayers have you rise
to be enfolded in a mass of light, if we die
how we've lived, then, sea-lover,
steward of a 100-gallon tank, I imagine you
sinking into the ocean's welcoming depths,
carried by gentle currents, accompanied
by sea horses and jewel-toned fish.

After Vesuvius

You died face down, arm up
as if to shield your eyes. Science
tells us you were seventeen, a slave,
pregnant. Years ago I learned
how a molten river covered your town,
preserving you for study.
But there was no lava.
Ash fell on Pompeii, lightly
at first and not alarming,
something you'd all felt before.
You had no idea
it would thicken, suffocating
anyone not already asphyxiated by gas.

The lava hit Herculaneum, a town
on the volcano's other side,
where families huddled at the port
planning escape, a tsunami
stopping the evacuation. We know the poor
by the ordinary color of their skeletons,
one child found with arms around a pet.
The rich, clutching safes and jewels,
in heat greater than three atomic bombs
were joined with their fortunes,
recognizable by their green bones.

Dead girl, though anonymous,
you're famous now,
seen and grieved by 10,000 visitors a day,
the same number that once filled
your thriving port town, a place
where slaves could buy their freedom
and join the upper class, perhaps
something you dreamed of
as you listened to the street bustle
while you worked, the first ash soft
and fluttery as the kicks of your child.

Leda

Babies need love
so I loved her
but she was a cold child,
all gold hair and entitlement,
stamping her majestic feet.
No surprise she made a nation burn.

I live a constricted life,
head down, jumping at shadows.
There are so many birds in the world.
Though I put out poisoned seed
to thin the flock, they find me
even in winter, even in sleep.
Dreams of beating wings,
the smother of feathers.

Why I Didn't Report

Because even while it's happening,
I'm working to forget,
numbing myself the way some spiders
paralyze their prey
                    (sweet balm of oblivion)

Years searching for an other self
                    not trapped in flesh (untouchable)

Because I wore (should not have worn)
stockings? shorts? a lime-green dress?
                    Details washed away
                    leaving only a stain.

Because he was a teacher.

Because it wasn't rape.

Because a girl learns
how the world will treat her body
                                        and her words.

Because months later when his name came up at dinner
and I told,
Dad kept eating, Mom laughed nervously,
then switched the topic.

Recently my aunt let me know
about their childhood trip to the movies,
how in the dark, the man
beside my mother snuck his hand
into her lap.

(Perhaps it wasn't laughter.
Perhaps she made a strangled sound.)

See, my memory's not believable,
too full of holes.

Two things I know for sure –
How his fingers marked me.
The soft click as he locked the door.

You Know You Should

Your uncle is dying,
the one you never liked,
so you perch stiffly
at the edge of his bed and steal
glances out the window
where the shrubs look like
your third grade gym class,
waiting for you to come out
and drop the ball.
You should kiss his cheek,
part of you wants to,
but the lie he told for years –
your sweet aunt sharpening, her laughter
never quite the same –
is lodged in your throat, impossible
to spit out or ignore, so you hold back,
shamed by your smallness,
able to do nothing more
than pour some melting ice cubes
from a pitcher to a paper cup.

Sunrise

Morning's mouth opens,
or is that my cats: *Feed us.*
So many hungers.

Tapping at the windowpane,
bare oak waiting for a bird.

Black Bird

(after Chris McCully)

I tread again into the bright forest
where the sharp sun's leaving
in her evening silks. Spying the trail,
I clumsily start,
crush berries red as desire.

Sight hardly helps, only finding
the earth's curve under the feet,
each rock, each texture rising.

Some things are still. Then the shallow darkness
solidifies around them in their starting upward –
circling, then quickening – all black birds.

There the prey is, trapped, a dun
bundle of fur, tail lifted,
quickly disappearing, quickly returning
as those eyes expected.

Now, noisily, the birds flap into the past,
tearing a slit in the still sky,
near rough clouds and shadows
cast by the sun's predictable descent.

First Warm Day

Cranky with overwintering,
we take our bikes to the park,
roll sleeves to let sun brighten our skin.
Swans hover in the lake's unfrozen
spots, pointed at by parents pushing strollers
around the loop.

Dizzy from pills we hope
will fix my blood, I huff
after my daughter as she races, dizzy
with new tween strength.

My husband brandishes a kite
with a magician's flourish.
The girls take turns, getting it to hover
and circle before each nose-bending crash.

I take my turn with low expectations,
but somehow today I sense
how to move and twist with each dip.
Effortless, this aiding flight.
I'm surprised
when the last twine unspools.

The girls whine hunger, so
I try to reign the kite in, but it
struggles like a fish,
clings stubbornly to the sky,
and I hesitate,
loathe to stop the soaring.

Coupled

Hoping a bike ride will banish
the tension between us, we strap on
our helmets and push off. The lake is
geeseful and sparkling.
Snatches of Spanish, Hebrew, Russian
as we pass and are passed. So many
families circle this path, an accident
seems imminent, but we make it
past the kayak rentals unscathed,
stop to watch two kites, fighter plane
and firefly, dip and rise.
Our sour feeling persists
despite the light-flecked water
with its pair of gliding swans.
Desperate, we reach for the news,
try to avoid a fight by hashing out
the war in Ukraine, mudslides, and a woman
who can now "enjoy a normal life" with
a vagina grown from her own tissue in a lab.

Twenty-Four Amazon Workers Hospitalized after Robot Co-Worker Sprays them with Bear Repellant

The story's tamer than the headline implies –
A fallen can. An accidental puncture. Not the running-amok
robot of my sci-fi nightmares. Still, didn't the brains
at Amazon – despite their understandable desire
for unpaid labor – spend their childhoods with the same
movies I did? Machines start out will-less, programmed
only to help, but inevitably some genius's
out-of-control creature will wreak havoc, the humans
killed fighting or fleeing, our species vanquished
by what we thought we could control.
What will earth be like once we're gone? Could the robots
do worse than our jealousies and extinctions, our land grabs
and lynchings, instruments of torture, lampshades
made with human skin? While a sweet, greeting-card
version of Mother Earth might mourn for us,
our demise won't rattle Gaia, in keeping
as it will be with Her ferocious devotion to balance
and growth. Perhaps, kinder than we deserve
in death as well as life, the fifty percent of wildlife
we've eliminated in the last forty years
will greet us with a nuzzle, though they might turn
their furred or feathered rumps and let us face oblivion alone.
Still, if the future does follow the expected B-movie script,
all isn't over for us. A band of plucky survivors
will find a ship and venture forth to colonize
another planet and restart the human race, hopefully,
though probably not, having learned
from past mistakes and doing better this time.

Hudson River Mile 28

The children pull on waders
and enter the river,
saltier here than at Haverstraw but less so
than at Piermont, which affects
what life they'll find in the net
they drag to the bank.
Counselors have a tank ready
for the wiggling fish we'll try to name
from a book. What shape are the fins?
If the tail splits, turn to page 30.
A small translucent one
dies in the transfer, is quickly
scooped out of sight. River advocates
believe the learning's worth it – *A relationship*
with even one creature
can open everything. They know
we only fight to protect what we love.
Across the water, a smudge of train
speeds people toward Manhattan.
Some children smash stones with mallets,
aiming for powder which, when wet,
acts as paint they'll use for portraits
of the fish. Other children
search for sea glass, former garbage
ground valuable.
A pit bull bounds after a stick,
returns soaked and triumphant,
then rolls in the sand. An old Golden
swims out, then farther out, white muzzle
turning the wrong way at his master's command.
Scared, the children stop and watch, parents
discuss diving in as the dog, blind (though we don't
know this then), paddles at a diagonal
away from shore.
Sometimes what we fear
doesn't happen, sorrow

waiting for another day. Counselors tell us
the once-toxic Hudson's now clean enough
for some fish to be eaten.
The retriever's owner wades out,
uses his voice to guide the dog home.

Gutted

Shingles, brick, wood, walls –
What makes a home?

Like a woman, a pipe
grows older.
Becomes less capable
of carrying others' shit.

A slow leak, months unnoticed.

We throw stuff in suitcases,
round up the animals.

The insurance company's a god.
We are granted a motel. Then an apartment.

Told to make a list of loss,
I write:
Extra arguments
Home Depot instead of sex
Missing the climbing tree
break out its short-lived blooms.

I omit the crumbling walls in my dreams.

The names of birds in our borrowed elm?
Impermanence, of course.
And *surrender*.

The house is a structure, painted blue.
It is not a metaphor.
It doesn't hold a marriage.

I will get a check,
new cabinets, a stove.

Yardless, the dog howls
behind our rented door.

Chagall's The Bridal Pair at the Eiffel Tower

Some guests still stand beneath the chuppah
watching the wedded pair set off
on what looks like a giant turkey
with a fiddler ensconced near its wing.
My groom and I left on a Harley, driving away
long enough for a photo op
before he dropped me back to meet him later
via safer transport. One might think
it a bad omen – taking different paths
before the marriage even starts,
but here we are, after two decades
of love and annoyances, him still riding,
me a short-trips-only passenger.
Chagall's bride looks less than thrilled
about the bird, though maybe she's noticed
that she's missing a hand, unless her gown
has hidden pockets, which would be even cooler
than the Keds my mom festooned with lace and pearls
so I could look fancy and still dance.
Who can really imagine what they're stepping into,
under a sun like a bloodshot eye,
can anticipate the previously-hidden
traits or floating cow heads that complicate everything.
Simpler, if less rich, to stay single,
like the figure reading a book in the tree's crown,
or the naked one who caught the bouquet
and now climbs skyward in celebration or escape.

Sometimes Clichés are True

To give someone your heart
is a metaphor for loving them,
though my husband has given his
to Chirag D. Badami, MD, whom he
doesn't love, and has just met,
and who will shortly crack
my husband's sternum and reach
for the pulsing muscle.

Out of the blue means suddenly,
as from the sky, the way I will
land, though right now I am
in the blue and listening
to the girl behind me whine,
Why can't you teach me?
and her mother answer, *Because*
it's hard. You just have to
know how to do it
and the daughter ask
Are there directions? and
the mother answer *No*.

My husband's blockage
wasn't out of the blue.
Still, finding out
he needs surgery now
knocked me sideways,
though not the way this plane
is knocking me sideways
as it lurches with *routine turbulence*.

Maybe by now my husband is under,
which means under the influence
of anesthesia, or under the surface
of waking consciousness and in
a drugged sea-world of dreams.

And maybe Dr. Badami, masked
and scrubbed, is ready with a scalpel –
my children's future hanging in the balance,
my husband's heart in his hands.

Finding Out Someone Stole My Daughter's Identity

Who wouldn't want
to be ten again, smooth-skinned
and nimble, revving up for junior high?
All your worst mistakes
in front of you. True, puberty's
trying – cliques, new
hips, and hormones – but this time
you'll have a driver's license
and all the knowledge
your wrinkled self suffered for.
You'll understand the mean girls'
crocodile smiles, cold-shoulder
the crude jock for a sweet computer
nerd who'll worship you and sell
his start-up for millions.
Feel the spring in your step as you
enter the crowded halls, drop
your loser jacket in a locker, and face
the party of growing up.
Sure this time you'll get it right.

Only as Sick

You're only as sick as your secrets, so we spilled
toward the well-being we hoped waited,
though Plath and Sexton confessed and weren't
helped, nor was my best friend's friend Elizabeth.
Liz mattered more to me
after she did it, my heart squeezed with unexpected grief,
trying to understand what took her pain
beyond the level we all lived with,
angst-filled and insecure, stuck in unrelenting
suburbs, then fleeing to punk clubs and hot
boys who kept us off-center and small.
They nodded out when we spoke or said *Sure, Babe*
and forgot. The music was enough, the music filled us,
though the boys made the music and in some songs
called us bitch or whore, we sang along, our faces scrunched
with longing. We spent hours analyzing the bands
and the boys though we never spoke of the power
we didn't have or how the world was –
hands clamped over female mouths –
and my best guess for why
Elizabeth turned on the gas
is that she wanted to choose her silence.

Fifteen

"There is a crack in everything, that's
how the night gets in." (Facebook post with typo)

My body fraught with fault lines

    Wound
             or door?

Old openness

                       new ache

Clove cigarettes   Strobed

                       dancing
                           in a
nightclub's throb

Hey ho, let's go

Night enters like a lover

       and says *now*

Sibling

When his mother beams at the baby,
his world shrinks to a closet
he'll never leave, crouched
among her silks and fur.

His sister's pink and fleshy toes. Her curls.
Her jump rope song.
Her report cards. So many ways
to erase him. Is any part
of him still here? He pulls wings
from a wiggling bug, pokes
his mother's dog with a toy sword.
His plastic soldiers wage war against
Barbies he steals from the intruder's room,
then returns, limbless, in shredded dresses.

He props a bucket of water to fall
on her head when she returns from college.
Calls her newborn daughter *troll*.

Nothing quiets her laughter - not money, beer.
Not his wife's kiss. His sister stalks him, mocking
him with her life.

Because he is a cloud,
irrelevant in summer's glare,
because his wife gives her breasts
to their son, he boycotts holidays, prays
his silence splinters like a bone in their throats.

Antigone

I perished how I lived –
my voice and desires smothered
by my brother's needs.

As a child, I resisted,
sulked when Mom gave him
the sweeter fruit, her brightest smiles.

Her looks of pain, more than
any scold or slap, trained me
to wait patiently behind him.

I acted from devotion, sure, but also –
Polynices' unburied corpse kept him
in our sight and conversation.

I hoped that when I filled
his mouth with earth
and left him underground,

I could walk home through the sweet
night air and there would
finally be enough for me.

Alcestis

I'm not selfless – it was die
for him or live with the guilt-inducing
final kiss I knew he'd insist on.
He was a master of the subtle stab,
the gentle shove, sticky demands
disguised as gifts. Dull,
suppressed by something I couldn't name,
I knew only constriction's ache.

Fever-bright, I drifted
between my failing body and delicious dream
till Hercules barged in,
all dumb muscle and helpfulness,
wrestled me away and dragged me
back into what passes for a life.

Fiction

Word-world, printed place of escape
from the terrors and tedium of flesh-and-blood life,
haven of loyal friendships,
passions that end well.
Even suffering's better – If a protagonist
gets cancer, we may learn about
her clogged feeding tube or the bruise
on her face from a fall, but only once.
The reader can assume
the next day's tube cleaning and fall.

Imagined war's a backdrop to the heroic
center tale, not decades of orphans or fractured
families trudging from the rubble.
The dystopian societies of literature will
fall in the end, a band of scrappy
rebels coupling off while they bring back democracy.
Even the most pessimistic novels
leave room for fans to rewrite
favorite characters into a happier last chapter.

A bestseller's dying teens realize – the world
wants us to notice it.
There's too much I don't want to see –
homeless couple slumped in the square, sad-eyed
photos of newly-extinct beasts.
Not to mention the countless quotidian annoyances –
stacked bills, unwashed pots, days wading through
the swamp of marital dissatisfaction.

Though she's mocked for being "too perfect,"
why not look to a Mary Sue for inspiration –
her loyalty and selflessness, her brains, her brawn,
her nick-of-time luck. Wardrobe flawless
for a ball or covert op. *Where's your mind?*
my yoga teacher asks. Mornings like today
when money looms over everything and the cat's

barfed on the rug, why not focus on Mary Sue
and her beneficence, my own heart
too small and wounded
for the gratitude my life deserves.

Invented Children

Stop putting me in poems,
my daughter commands.
My flesh and blood daughter.
Her details, the triumphs and struggles
of her life, are hers. I won't poach.
But the all-encompassing morass
of motherhood is mine,

so I make up offspring who won't mind
sharing their loose teeth and cute sayings,
their puberty, ambitions, untied shoes.

Inspired by her fictitious first dance,
his failed math test, I ruthlessly expose
the rooms in my maternal heart.
His cowlick, so like my father's,
sparks a sonnet. Her softball triumph
swells into rhyme.

Free to tell everything,
even what's embarrassing,
I do,
then, ready to return
to my real family,
I tuck them under covers.

Daedulus

Of course I warned him.
It's a father's job to curb enthusiasm,
to blanket possibility with fear.
Not too low, the waves will wet
your feathers, nor too high --
the sun may melt your wings' wax seal.
I gave these words my sternest tone.

My heart has never healed,
grief vast as the sea
that claimed him.

Still, those first minutes
as he soared, my spirit
followed, swelling
with the potency of youth,
trusting the world's benevolence,
thinking that a man
could join the gods in flight
and there'd be no bad luck
or scientific law to slap him down.

Getting Ready for the March

Writing my phone number in Sharpie
on my daughter's arm,
I try not to see
other numbers on Jewish skin.

Election Cycle

I. One Day Before the Election

The country readies like a hunter, crouched,
while children play in wind-whirled leaves
and scared shoppers wipe boxes with bleach.
Teens obsess about death
without believing in it.
Radios drone poll numbers and predictions.
Hope alternates with terror
like a billboard blinking between ads.
Even the dog cuts her night walk short,
straining back toward our familiar street
under a moon that shows us
her whole face, inscrutable
and light years from the nearest star.

II. "Your Life Can Change In An Instant"

they say, and they're right –
a chance meeting in a café,
a physician calling with lab results.
An election.
I stand in a line
that curves like snakes on flags
the thugs waved when they blocked the bridge,
police on the scene doing nothing.
Though my doctor told me,
*Sleep as much as possible, stay
off your feet,* nothing will stop me
from filling in ovals with a prayer.
The line shuffles forward over stones
engraved with names of somebody's
beloved dead, a few half-covered
with dull leaves that dropped
before they had a chance to blaze.

III. Waiting for the Final Results

Four years ago we watched the map bleed red,
stain spreading till I sent my kids
to bed, aborting their school assignment
to color the states. That election's ghost
chills our home despite the thermostat's number.
Right now, he's ahead again.
What is a country anyway?
What are my neighbors?
I'm not a Buddhist, never believed
the answer was to let desires drop away like leaves,
leaving the stark, accepting soul. They say
pain comes from resisting what is.
Nails bitten, jaw clenched, my body
offers proof. Dragged out by the dog, I glare
at other walkers, looking for a smile
or a clear brow to indicate
they're on the other side. My puppy
doesn't care, she wags at everyone,
her skilled nose leading me
into whatever the future will be.

IV. November 7, 2020

Pulling weeds in the yard, I hear
a wordless, full-throated holler
and nudge my daughter,
fenced inside her headphones. *I think he
won.* A moment later, the street erupts.
William Burroughs said, *Perhaps all pleasure
is relief,* and what I'm feeling and see
mirrored in the faces of flag-waving neighbors

isn't like the ecstasy from a Lotto win, or
the heart-bursting bliss of new parenthood.
Instead, we share the giddy exhale when a car
that almost hits you stops in time, or a loved one,
lost for days in fever-dream, wakes up
to take a few shaky-handed spoonfuls of broth.

V. No Poem

Matters as much
as the news we hear
and cheer and cry
and finally, after four years,
breathe.

VI. Newt Gingritch Claims 150,000 Dead People Voted

I want to believe him,
to imagine the dead marking ovals
or pulling levers with transparent hands.
Where did they go after, their "I Voted" stickers
stuck to whatever they were buried in?
Were they allowed back
only for this one act, or could they stay,
pick up plastics from the beach or push
a child from the path of a car? Were they confined
to the state they died in, or could they cross lines?
Thank you, Newt, for giving me the image
of my mother helping choose the first female V.P.
Perhaps she's on her way to my house now.
I'll put the kettle on, make sure her favorite cup is clean.

VII. Insurrection Snapshots

Words aren't swords, or bombs,
gunpowder, rifles, dragons.
Not a scaffold with a waiting noose.
Words aren't religion, airplanes,
torn-out panic buttons,
flagpoles or fire extinguishers.
Not a zip tie. Not a wick.
Just the flame.

*

Rioters climb through the broken glass.
Just one bullet, roses blooming
from the hole in one white throat.

From mad rush to single-file
when they see the velvet ropes – some instinct
or manners turns the mob obedient,
gives the prey essential
seconds to escape.

*

A rioter brags his sharpened flagpole
is for "someone special."
Others yell for Pence, Pelosi, AOC,
their "hidden" offices
circled on maps.

*

Praise to the officers, outnumbered and battered.
Praise to the clerk who thought to grab the votes.
Praise to the selfie-posting killers' desire for fame.
Praise to crews who soap the shit-stained halls.

*

Woman with a Don't Tread on Me banner
trampled to death.
Rioter tasers himself in the groin.
Though reporters mock the fur-clad people
as cosplayers, my daughter corrects,
That's live-action role play.

*

Blood and feces scrubbed away,
already the story's changing.
Lies fester in the aftermath.
Rage-filled gun buyers prepare for the next round.
The horned one eats organic food in jail.

After the Doctor Appointment

Scared to leave this world, I fail
to see it, retreating into
fantasies of triumph or loss.
Not blinded by fear, but blurred.
The flowers on my walk home smudge
to splotches. No petals or stamens,
no delightful Latin names. Foggy, I trudge
until I'm startled by a bush on fire.

A closer look reveals not flame,
but cardinal, so flagrantly scarlet, so blindingly
bright, I can't look away.
Smacked back to awareness, I reenter
my body. Liver plodding on as best it can, heart
driven toward wholeness by desire.

A Blood Test Reveals That I'm CT

(Variation in the IL28B gene is a strong predictor of treatment response. Patients with CC fare the best, TT the worst, and CT in between. The C mutation is passed by an ancestor who survived a killer flu.)

I'm grateful, but to whom?
Peasant forebears?
The almost mythic great great somebody
who fled from Russian soldiers in a wagon
full of hay? One of Mom's grandmothers –
Big Bubbi or Little Bubbi, one tiny and stern,
the other massive, grinning in grainy snapshots?

How many generations back did someone
rise up from a sickbed
with this weapon in their DNA?

Perhaps my father's father
carried it across the ocean,
docking at Ellis Island with a love
for cats and knack for losing
money. More probable,
the dour Germans on his mother's side.
Easy to imagine one of them lifting
a wide hand, refusing to die, while
other villagers dropped like flies.

Whoever you were, I thank you
for this fraction of a cure,
this half a chance.

Cure

Life was handed back to me,
a loaf of dark bread.
Sun-pools on the floor, the doctor
smiling. How to reawaken
appetites fear-dampened
for years. Are my teeth
sharp enough to take the gift?

Miami Elegy

You were the no-rules relatives,
the once-a-year Florida treat.
Lizards on the door-screens,
a creek out back. Black pig
in your neighbor's yard. The Parrot Jungle's
bright splotches of bird.

No bedtime, kids literally
climbing the walls
(though I was too timid to try), my cousin
eating peanut butter from the jar.

Uncle, you left your big-deal job
at the office, bowed to your wife's
bossy efficiency, were something
I haven't seen since – a humble lawyer.

Afternoons sunburning
on The Barnacle Billy
while the boys water-skied, petrol
mixing with the odor of the sea.

Now you're starving – the lump
that stops you from swallowing
also blocking a feeding tube, ironic
for one who loved to eat. Once
my mother marveled, *They start
talking about dinner before breakfast!*

The proverb instructs, *roots and wings*
and you succeeded, your kids grounded
and soaring, even the late-bloomer
finally set. Two generations fly back
to plant themselves around
your bed and share memories,
trying to nourish you with words.

What of the Moon

How to find words
worthy of trees' chopped-down bodies,
to find the place where stanzas dart,
bright as fish beneath the trash-strewn ocean
of everyday speech?

Earnestness is not enough.
A political slogan
isn't poetry, though rarely
a poem will hatch and flutter
from the shell of its ideals.
The arc a figure makes
falling from a roof isn't poetry.
My suffering isn't poetry,
nor is yours.

A fire-scarred forest
isn't poetry, though the remaining
finches' gold comes close.
Their song, closer.
Closer still, the silence
when the singing stops.

Magicicada

Louder than a lawnmower,
with an other-worldly metal buzz,

the males call. These few weeks
for a lifetime of song.

The shock of their red eyes
on a gray day.

How did they know when to rise?
Newly-hatched, they're milky yellow,

then the wings unfold
and darken as they dry.

Clumsy fliers at first,
then picking up speed.

Our whole town buzzes with them,
children giddy, adults stopping to stare.

You don't have to be good,
the famous poet insists

in her poem about following desire.
So let's not judge the Lab puppy

who gulps dozens on daily walks.
Her one chance

for this particular pleasure.
When they return, I'll be

my mother's age
when she died.

Now the full moon mothers me
with watchfulness and absence,

silvers the cicada's holes,
their outworn skins.

"The Future Isn't What it Used to Be"

But it's the one we're falling into, so why not
charge our electronic devices
and get on with it? Let your daughter mock
the vinyl discs that carried you
to paradise. Save nostalgia
for high school reunions and 12-Step meetings.
Admit the beauty "back then"
had its own snares. Are the kids
exhausting their thumbs in substitutes
for talking really more disconnected
than you, twirling in your parents' kitchen,
phone cord wrapping like a snake
around your awkward body?
Bodies are the same, though of course
yours was firmer in that past
which was then the present. Which your
daughter will realize someday, now twisting
in the mirror, transfixed
by imaginary flaws. Be honest – isn't the future,
however lacking, a match for
your own confused youth
when you sang with loneliness,
smearing sweet potato on your face
to get more kisses from the dog?

Stores Sell Padded Bras for Toddlers

I've never met an angel, but I know
fear better than I understand gravity,

phenomenon that keeps us from careening
into the waiting abyss. Are all the calm folks

angel-touched and anchored?
Whatever light I'm missing,

I know terror
has its own wings. How they beat

in the belly, teach
the law of boy and prey.

What would it feel like
to be a woman, and whole?

Years After Loss,

The world forms a scar,
a thick, dulling skin
unnoticed by most.
For them, the river
still sparkles, the stomach
still constricts with fearful joy
to see a rollercoaster
loop screaming patrons
into the sky.

Maybe it's not the world.
My eyes turn everything
to someone showering
behind frosted glass,
even children, even
a butterfly drinking a turtle's tears.

At least when my heart was broken,
it was open.

I Always Smile at Obese People in the Gym

Everyone's working on something,
my apraxic daughter's teacher tells
the kids who ask about her speech.
In our pretend school, my daughter
taps her pointer and announces,
We only sing when you're absent.
Why can't I, who treasures and tingles to music,
match my voice to what I hear?
I'd hate that if it were me, a friend
commiserates, then casually mentions
his perfect pitch. So when I see
a fleshy woman sweating
on a snail's pace treadmill
or a round man huffing with a trainer, I raise
my water bottle to our myriad
flavors of struggle.
Perhaps our limits could
replace the zodiac as conversation starters –
Can't draw? Neither can my husband
or *You're a no sense of direction, too!*
What we label loses force,
old gods stripped of power
when their names are spoken, just as,
to cut the risk of disappointment and divorce,
some couples expose their flaws
in prenuptial "Shadow Ceremonies"
where they hire clergy, dress in
sloppy clothes and vow
to be controlling and short-tempered
or *to flirt with other men.*

Sentencing

After the prison dream
I wake foggy, off-balance,
surprised by the touch of the cat.

Rarely are there bars, though I know
the grey walls hold me. Often I'm running,
chased down halls that narrow and shift.
My legs are clumsy, my shoes
too small. Sometimes I turn myself in,
dream-body brittle and numb. Officials talk loudly
about sentencing. Mom is usually
beside me with a suitcase, or trying
to smuggle in lunch.

I can go months without coming here,
then visit twice in a week.

When the alarm rings, I'm relieved
if it's raining. My heaviness
congruent. The bad mood
lasts, along with a sense
of having left something important behind
that my body strains
back toward, even as I plod
through the possibilities of my
present-tense life.

The Dream Book hands me black and white
assurances – *You're not just the protagonist,*
but all the other elements as well – the glass door
I shuffle toward to surrender, the fat guard who leers
at my blond hair. I'm my mother and the tissue
she sobs into, then shoves crumpled into her purse.
I'm the heavy door that clangs shut, and the purple
Chevy driving slowly away.

Train

Old cars rattle, tilt
at each curve. Through smudged windows,
a line of trees, stiff as bridesmaids.
We're all too close.

Music leaks from headphones
into air thick with chicken and fries.
Most heads bow
over screens.

An expensively-dressed couple
try to figure out where to get off.
Their bickering starts low, rises.
I listen without wanting to, scrunched

down in the blue naugahyde seat.
In front of me, two hippies kiss.
How long before they slide
into sweet spite of tits and tats?

Stations pass, predictable
as grievance follows need.
An almost-empty can rolls
down the aisle, dribbling Coke,

is finally halted by a white sandal.
Bright posters show island getaways,
fake breasts, a giant diamond
shooting air-brushed lines of light.

Details

The condition of the truck's brakes
when the child dashes to retrieve an errant ball

Snow masking
a patch of ice

An open can
that lures a rabid raccoon to the tent

The boots the new girl
chooses for the party

Chemicals in the water
binding to chemicals in the food

can change everything.

When the adolescent
preens in a pink bikini,

how does her stepfather respond?
What if the full-breasted girl

looks older than twelve?
So much is determined by

whether he drank orange juice
or beer with lunch.

Small things
rub against each other.

Brakes. Bikini. Beer. An open can.
A girl. What's underneath a mask.

Blocked
(after Vievee Francis)

Such thick things – a black wool coat,
the stare of one eye fixed upon another staring
eye, the stench of cologne in the air
after the moon cools everything to soothing
blur. The barriers are solid, believe me –
a steel wall, complex and light-blocking, between wanting
and feeling full. I reach for your chest,
grab to awaken the tough muscle
freed now from dense fabric
once sealed like an eviction notice I open, then burn.

Outsider Cento

Music is somebody arguing with God. It's about
a mixture of two cold things
in the dead tongues of saints.

Some days I impersonate myself
clutching my freedom, trusting for surest friend
orange juice and chocolate bars. The color red
and a whistling dove.

Because someone wasn't paying attention
again the word's been stolen,
like the music in old music boxes, when time itself slows
down in them.

(Made with lines from the anthology, *Outsider: Poems about Exiles,
Rebels, and Renegades*, edited by Laureanne Bosselar)

Eight Minutes, Forty-Six Seconds

(i.m. George Floyd)

Five hundred twenty-six seconds.
Time in which an athlete
can run a mile and a half.
A couple can have rushed,
workday-morning sex.
A teacher can teach about the stars.
A killer can keep his knee
on the neck of a man.

Bystanders take videos,
their raised phones weapons
against erasure. The athlete huffs toward the line.
The couple finish, kiss, and dress, smiling.
The bystanders beg and are ignored.
The teacher is talking about gas and plasma,
how the earth's movement creates
what we see as twinkling.

Now some cities burn, years
of bitter repetition going up in flames,
grief heavy as the boots that shatter glass.
Other protestors peacefully
sit in the street repeating his name.
For nine minutes, traffic stopped.
The lovers sit at separate cubicles.
The teacher explains what glows in darkness
is the light from those that died.

Poem for Kendrick Castillo

You don't look like the image of "hero,"
unlike the brawny blond athlete who tackled
the last shooter, though as much as the middle-aged lady
who threw herself in front of the rabbi.
Sorry to make you share this poem
with others, but there are so many and we need
to conserve the trees we have left.
Maybe soon we'll just swap out names
the way Elton John
recycled Marilyn's song for Diana.

We say the dead live on
in their actions. So you persist
in other students – their bodies intact
because you lunged – almost ready
to throw caps in the air
and head into the rest of their lives.
Maybe this comforts your parents,
everyone still lauding your courage,
though you'll get knocked off
the news soon enough. One grief
flowing into the next. Children
sitting in classrooms. The next
gun shining somewhere, loaded.

There Is No Gun

There is no gun in this poem.
No politicians. No money.
The children sit in classrooms. If a boy
pulls the fire alarm, it's a dumb prank.
The closets are stuffed with buckets
and brooms.The children's blood
is under their skin. Some are learning
how it pumps from heart to artery to vein.

There are no heroes,
though teachers unpack books
they've paid for and the unthanked janitor
mops vomit in the hall.
The coach wonders which drills
will bring his team to victory,
not how many bodies
his bulk can shield. The news crews
are elsewhere with their helicopters and headlines.

Some kids play violent video games.
Some are angry and attack
with fists or catty Snapchat posts.
There is no AR-15. No fixed adjustable
front and rear iron sights. No
30-round staggered-column detachable
box magazine. No 25 rounds in 2.5 seconds.
The bell rings in this poem.
Children grab their backpacks and head home.

July, 2018

Because *politics can make kids anxious,*
I say nothing to my daughters
about the migrants
as we stand on the roof awaiting fireworks,
delighting in how beautiful the sky looks
as cobalt bleeds into pink.
All week the media's been stuck on
twelve Thai soccer players trapped in a cave.
The danger! The oxygen! Hourly updates.
One brief mention
that activists were told to stop protesting
outside facilities where children wait in cages,
the well-intentioned chanting
just another flavor of terror.
Those heroic divers! The forecast of rain!
The roof deck is crowded.
The detention centers are crowded.
Hats, flags, streamers – so much red, white, and blue.
As the finale begins, a thick
cloud drifts over the blossoming light,
moving like an eclipse until
only a sliver is visible.
Boats honk in the bay. The boys and their coach
rescued! Half the migrant kids under age five,
court-ordered returned to their families,
haven't been. The parents *difficult to locate,*
some deported. The boys invited, but too weak,
to attend The World Cup. Teary, I pack
trunks for camp. Protein bars, water shoes, extra
sunblock. The privilege to miss my children
for two weeks. *I'll write every other day.* A barefoot
one-year-old's compelled to represent himself in court.

September 11, 2015

In the gym, people work
to make their bodies stronger and more beautiful,
perhaps strive for longer life.
Attached to the bike I'm riding,
a TV and no way to turn it off. Serena
has beaten Venus, will play
today in the semifinals.

At the screen's bottom, the dead:
beside each photograph,
a name, age, place of residence.
Why those details?
Why not their favorite joke,
something they loved?
I watch the faces for clues –
was that man a banker?
Someone on one of the planes?

(I will put no names in this poem
since I lack space to list them all.)

Many seem like i.d. photos – stiff, unsmiling, though
in a few, the subject snuggles a child
or beams in a cap and gown.
When the network has no photo,
they show an American flag.

My simulated hills are done.
The bike's lights flash *Congratulations*.
I stay seated, watch more of the doomed
scroll by – his wry expression, her shy eyes –
then, like the living can,
I get up and walk away.

All Four Were Removed Alive

The mail is full of concern.
Are your windows letting money out?
Does snoring interfere with sex?
Termites can destroy your home's foundation.
It has come to our attention
that you might be diabetic.
Like a submissive,
controlling lover, one letter cajoles,
You haven't yet responded to our survey. Please
tell us how we can better serve your needs.

What are my needs today, washing breakfast dishes
while the birds conduct discussions
and newscasters deliver the latest outrage?
Knowing even if I turn it off,
there's no way to turn it off.

Reaching for gratitude as an antidote,
I start with the obvious - that I'm not a mother
ripped from her children,
that I live here and not in one of the countries
families are fleeing from.
And the smaller stuff - though I need to watch
my sugar intake, I'm not diabetic,
and despite my husband's snoring
breaking up my sleep, our passion's fine.

The radio offers another gem -
at least I'm not the woman
who thought her itchy, painful eyes
were caused by grains of sand
but found out she had
bees beneath her eyelids
feeding on her tears.

Poem in Which I Try Not to Mention the IRS

With whom I've been spending hours
on the phone, struggling
to fix their mistake until finally
told *This department doesn't*
fix mistakes, we help you
work around them.
There are so many things
more worthy of attention –
strawberries, string, sky, the limpid
eyes of cows. If I'm wanting
someone to take shots at,
there are better targets,
like the House Republicans,
who blocked the Equal Pay for Women bill
a third time, calling it *condescending*
to the ladies and *a distraction*
from failed economic policy. Still, after
reading *Gratitude is as dependable*
as suffering, I'm resolved
to celebrate. Let me go outside,
drink in the unfolding
gold of nascent daffodils before
our neighbors' overzealous lawn service
chops off their heads.

Even So

There's nothing to say about Spring
that hasn't been written before.
Still, I offer this particular
pit bull – her frantic laps of celebration,
her devotional rolling. Squeaks
from her rubber bone blend
with the birds' chatter. Snow-lost
fetch-balls have defrosted, our lawn
blossoming with yellow, pink, and orange spheres.

Alison Stone has published seven full-length collections, *Zombies at the Disco* (Jacar Press, 2020), *Caught in the Myth* (NYQ Books, 2019), *Dazzle* (Jacar Press, 2017), *Masterplan,* a book of collaborative poems with Eric Greinke (Presa Press, 2018)*, Ordinary Magic,* (NYQ Books, 2016), *Dangerous Enough* (Presa Press 2014), and *They Sing at Midnight,* which won the 2003 Many Mountains Moving Poetry Award; as well as three chapbooks. Her poems have appeared in *The Paris Review, Poetry, Ploughshares, Barrow Street, Poet Lore,* and many other journals and anthologies. She has been awarded *Poetry*'s Frederick Bock Prize and *New York Quarterly*'s Madeline Sadin Award. She was Writer in Residence at LitSpace St. Pete. She is also a painter and the creator of The Stone Tarot. A licensed psychotherapist, she has private practices in NYC and Nyack. www.stonepoetry.org www.stonetarot.com. YouTube – Alison Stone Poetry.